IMAGES OF ENGLAND

CREWS HOLE
SPEEDWELL
AND ST GEORGE

IMAGES OF ENGLAND

CREWS HOLE
SPEEDWELL
AND ST GEORGE

DAVE STEPHENSON, ANDY JONES,
JILL WILLMOTT AND DAVID CHEESLEY

TEMPUS

Frontispiece: St Michael's church, Two Mile Hill. The church dates from 1848 and there are some very interesting graves in the churchyard. One such is the grave of Private Potter (see pages 107–108).

First published 2003

Tempus Publishing Limited
The Mill, Brimscombe Port,
Stroud, Gloucestershire, GL5 2QG

www.tempus-publishing.com

British Library Cataloguing in Publication Data.
A catalogue record for this book is available from the British Library.

ISBN 0 7524 2948 5

Typesetting and origination by Tempus Publishing Limited
Printed in Great Britain by Midway Colour Print, Wiltshire

Contents

	Acknowledgements	6
one	Netham	7
two	Crews Hole	17
three	St George	49
four	Speedwell	83
five	Historical Adverts and Miscellaneous	121

Acknowledgements

We would like to thank Tony Williams, John Merrett, Bet Whitlock, Brian Gosney, Gordon and Pauline Elliott, Don Goddard, Colin Chadwick, Jack Britton, Gwen Watson, Hanham Local History Society, Mrs F. Gearing, Mrs M. Smith, Reg Gregory, Neil Shortman, Ray Dark, David Gore, David Harrison, Brian Hodges, Jean and Clive Short, Mary Sheppard, Harry Milson, Violet Britton, Gordon Feaver, Pat Brain, Marion Sheppard, Alice Weymouth, Samuel Loxton, Doreen Hole, William Sanigar, Barbara Maggs, Maurice Pittman, James Russell, Mike Hooper, John Saysall, George White, Donald Speirs, Mike Tozer, Bernard Merrick, Alan Sawyer, Brian Haskins, Tony Brake, Bernard Joy, Gordon Worgan, Esme Bryant, Les Howard, H.B. Priestley, Doctor Fryer, Miss Floss, Charlotte Webb, Pauline Luscombe, William Hicks, Mrs Prigg, Syd and Audrey Marks, John Cornwell, Garry Atterton, James Cole, Mike Baker, Mr Jones, Jim McNeil, Harold Dancey, Alan Freke, F.C. Blampied, George Gardiner (Snr), Edna Williams, Ernie Haste, Amy Sutton, Bristol Library Services, Denise Banwell, Pip Sheard, Andy Parsons, Mike Poole, the *Bristol Evening Post*, ICI.

Publications consulted:
  St Anne's, Bristol, Winchester, E.
  Stories of King's Chase, Elliott, G. and Snell, J.
  City Pit, Moss, F.
  Killed in a Coalpit, Lindergaard, D.P.
  Crofts End 1895-1995 (compiled by congregation)
  Journeying into Openness, Hares, B.

Very special thanks to the late Mrs Edna Williams of Dale Street, St George; Alice Weymouth of Crews Hole; and William Nethercott for his memories of the Civil Defence Corps at Netham.

one

Netham

The Netham lock-keeper's cottage, which dates from the
completion of the Feeder Canal in 1809. A cast-iron plaque above
the door read: 'BUILDING 1/BRISTOL DOCKS'. The actual
lock was built of Pennant stone with two sets of timber lock gates.
Note the prominent Port of Bristol notice board.

From the Feeder Canal, the Netham chemical works dominated the approach into Crews Hole. Evolving from the 1860s, it was an east Bristol industrial giant, with monumental chimneys towering over a jumble of assorted structures, including furnaces and steam cranes. It boasted an elaborate light tramway network, which serviced a vast, sprawling waste tip that stretched to Barton Hill. To the south the Feeder Canal and the River Avon were vital to the operation. Two groups of men, the 'process workers' and the 'yard men' toiled in this huge, dark labyrinth of a works.

In the 1880s a *Bristol Times and Mirror* reporter visited the plant and his report gave a graphic account of the reality of this great alkali works.

> 'These works, which are situated at Crews Hole, a short distance from the city, are very extensive. In fact they cover more ground than any other manufactory in this neighbourhood. When we say that nearly forty acres are required for the purpose of the business, that upon this there is built over a mile of shedding, that about 400 workpeople are employed, a tolerably good idea of the extent of the concern may be gathered.
>
> It is all hard, grimy reality. The huge mounds of refuse that put one in mind of miniature mountains, the tall brick chimneys, the great wooden structures, black with creosote, that rise here and there like castles, the long rows of shedding. The scene has nothing aesthetic or poetical about it – and the visitor must be prepared accordingly.'

In 1927 the Netham works became part of the ICI group. Although the plant closed down in 1949, the site was so extensive that only over many years were the bewildering structures of the plant finally removed, some still being visible in 1982. The mass of buildings included many store sheds with galvanised iron roofs, dilapidated timber and brick structures, oxygen and petrol stores, tanks, loading bays and corrugated iron storage areas. In addition the works had its own recreation ground, allotments, quarry and, across the Avon, railway sidings.

The 1950s saw a period of transition for Netham. The production of chemicals had ceased but evidence of the vast works was all around. A section of the site remained as a chemical depot, while the council began the task of taming the huge waste heap known locally as the 'brillos'. It was amongst this 'wilderness of tips' that the post-war Civil Defence Corps established a divisional HQ and rescue training ground. Utilising some of the old structures of the works and the wild nature of the landscape, one of the finest rescue training centres in the United Kingdom was created between 1952 and 1956.

With a fair chunk of the ICI site at their disposal, the Civil Defence Corps expanded their operations at Netham. Chain-link fencing and concrete posts eventually separated the training ground from the land to the west. Here the council decided to level and grass over the waste chemical tip. Work started in 1954 but throughout the 1950s it was not clear what the final outcome would be. Some early plans indicated a more formal type of park but by 1962, the cheaper option of a stark playing field had won the day.

Civil Defence operations at Netham were abandoned from 1965. This coincided with plans to develop a stadium at Netham. Besides the cost and technical difficulties, one major problem was the unsuitability of the Netham Road. In 1968 the city engineer stated that 'the gradient, width and alignment of Netham Road are extremely unsatisfactory and an early improvement is desirable'.

It was not until summer 1982 that work was started to realign Netham Road. A sweeping new highway was cut through the site of the old works buildings, linking the lower Netham Road with Blackswarth Road. The demolition of the final four buildings of the works marked the end of a process that had started in 1949. The new link road was called Fireclay Road, a name reflecting the industrial heritage of the Netham/Crews Hole area.

The Feeder Canal and the Netham Lock from a drawing by the famous Bristol illustrator Samuel Loxton, dated 1913. The Netham Lock is the upstream entrance to the Feeder Canal and the Floating Harbour. The buildings on the left were part of the Netham United Alkali chemical works (later ICI). Off to the right was the Netham steel works of John Lysaght.

Almost the same view fifty-five years later. In the distance are the buildings of Mardon Son & Hall, printers. The three tall chimneys belong to the immense St Anne's Board Mill, which, like Mardon's was part of the Imperial Group at this time. The tallest chimney – touching 300 feet – was visible for miles around.

The Netham bridge over the lock, late 1950s. A milk lorry crosses into Netham Road with the bleak landscape of the former chemical waste tip off left. On the right are former ICI buildings, which at this time were being used by the Civil Defence Corps. The canal bridge has been rebuilt several times and in 1974 a second Bailey-type bridge was added to ease the traffic flow across the lock.

The alkali works at Netham had its own fire brigade, as a fire at any large industrial complex could develop into a serious disaster. Industrial brigades competed against each other. The Netham team sit proudly with a cup they won in the early 1900s.

The distinctive 1930s New Brislington bridge with the ICI Netham works in the background, 25 August 1949. The chimney was known as the 'Netham Monster' and was one of the tallest ever seen in Bristol. However, by this time it had been considerably reduced in height pending demolition.

Members of the Civil Defence Corps attend a presentation at their Netham headquarters in the 1950s. Mr Nethercott, who was in charge of CDC Netham is in the centre left of the picture. After sterling service during the Second World War, the Civil Defence Corps was reformed in 1949. Off to the left was the HQ building, the old main office of the ICI works. This was a fairly substantial structure, mainly brick but with part-rubble walls and a slate and tile roof. It contained a hall and numerous rooms.

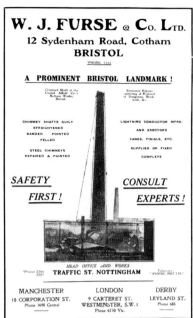

Left: Netham Road in the 1970s, looking to the New Brislington bridge. The stone walls are the remains of buildings from the chemical factory. Note part of a window opening, filled in with concrete blocks. *Right*: An unusual advertisement for W.J. Furse & Co. Ltd showing the well-known chimney shaft at the United Alkali Company's Netham works, which they had repaired.

The original Brislington bridge, built by John Lysaght. In the background is part of the Netham ICI works complex. The bridge replaced an earlier ferry service. It was replaced in the 1930s by the present concrete structure.

Local kids at the Netham Civil Defence training centre. These lads appear to be taking a break from an exercise. At Netham, specially built 'damaged buildings' were erected for use in rescue training exercises. Mock two-storey houses and tunnels were used to test the various Civil Defence teams. An old ICI building known as the 'south building' was used as a mess room, 'make-up' room and store. The Netham training ground was officially opened in March 1953.

The Civil Defence Corps used the old ICI garages for the storage of a range of rescue vehicles. This view is from the garage compound towards the Netham Cooperage, the works of the Western Salvage Company and the houses in the middle of Netham Road. By the late 1960s, all evidence of Civil Defence operations at Netham had been removed. The site remained rather wild until it was grassed over, becoming part of the playing fields.

The Wagon and Horses, Netham Road. This pub was used by the workers of the Netham chemical works. Despite a 'no drinking at work' rule brought in by manager Philip Worsley, the Wagon and Horses was seen as an essential part of the works. It originally had an attached brew house and a skittle alley. The much-modified building is still in existence, although it had closed as a public house by the mid-1960s.

View from Arlington Road looking across the River Avon to the ICI Netham works. Next to the stack are the massive chemical-condensing towers. The picture dates from 25 August 1949.

July 1989. In the foreground is the newspaper recycling depot at the bottom of Netham Road. In the background, Mardon's factory is in the process of being demolished.

In summer 1982 a sweeping new link road was cut, connecting Netham Road (in the foreground) with Blackswarth Road. Up to this time, the lower Netham Road remained essentially the same narrow, steep road that it had been when it threaded its way through the middle of the chemical works. Plans for a new Netham Road had first surfaced in the 1950s.

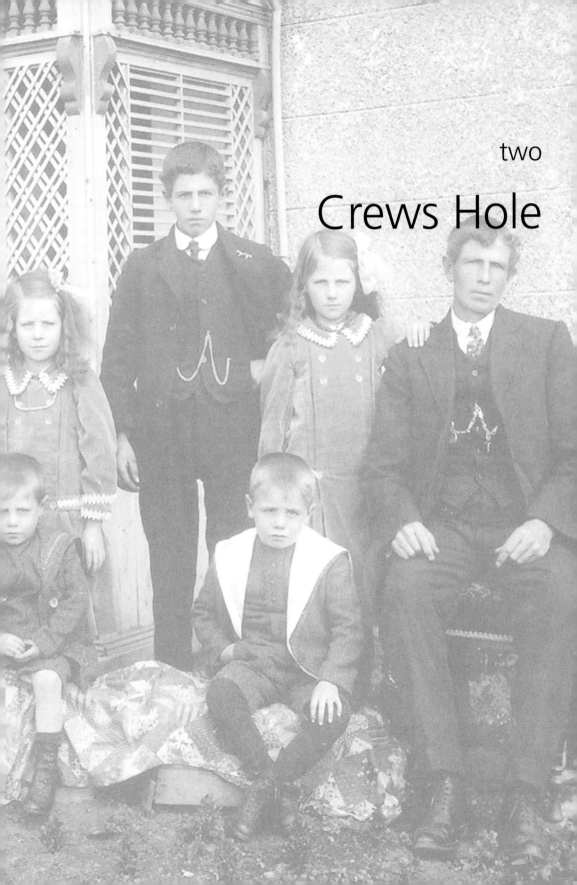

two

Crews Hole

Crews Hole. A unique Bristol landscape, $2\frac{1}{2}$ miles east of the city centre. The Troopers Hill chimney has been a landmark for over 200 years.

Crews Hole takes its name from Cruses Cottages, which once stood on the opposite side of the river. The Cruse family practically owned most of the land there. From Cruse came Screws Hole, and finally Crews Hole. However, there is another theory: that the area took its name from the crews of old sailing ships who sheltered here from the dreaded press gangs. It is also to Crews Hole that persecuted Baptists fled from Bristol. It is said that they cut steps or terraces into the hillside in 1682 to serve as a gallery for their congregation. Lookouts were posted at the top of the hill to watch for the sheriff or a mob.

Although the mining of mineral deposits – primarily coal, sandstone and lead – had been carried out in the area from at least the Middle Ages, the Bristol Brass Company brought new industry to the area in 1710, and by 1724 there were twenty-four furnaces operating in Crews Hole. This rose to forty-nine and production continued until 1828, when the derelict mills were sold.

A copper works stood nearby at Conham, built in around 1696. It was later sold to the Bristol Brass Company. Much later the site was used as a council rubbish tip. Parts of these old works can still be seen in the woods.

Slag blocks made at Crews Hole still survive throughout Bristol, incorporated into many walls and houses. The Black Castle at Brislington is the best example of a building made with these blocks.

Between 1766 and 1803 there were three glasshouses here, two of which produced soap. Also here was the Bristol Fire Clay Co., producing almost unbreakable bricks. The company operated from the 1880s until the early 1900s. The Crown Clay Co. was another firm making firebricks, but they also produced sanitary pipes and terracotta ware from about the same date.

In Victorian times, Crews Hole was compared to the north Devon village of Clovelly, as both were steep, with ranks of cottages that tumble down lanes and narrow roads to the waterfront. In contrast with this idyllic scene was the intense concentration of industry making it the Avonmouth of its day. Employment attracted workers, and short terraces of dwellings were built amongst the scattering of earlier cottages. A relatively secluded and independent community grew, its distinct character reflecting the area's setting, development and history.

The Feeder Canal changed the River Avon, which had been a tidal river up to this point. At low tide the ferry was turned into a floating bridge, parked in the middle with planks to the bank on each side.

Another force for change in the village was the tar works. In 1843, William Butler was the manager of this tar works owned by Roberts and Daines. He had previously worked with Brunel on the Great Western Railway. Brunel needed products to protect the wooden sleepers under the railway tracks. We are sure Brunel had some connection with this plant, if only in an advisory capacity.

In 1863 a fire broke out, nearly destroying the plant. The owners, fearful of the fire risks, sold out to William Butler, who then gave his name to the factory. Another fire broke out in 1897, killing one of its employees. It was described at the time as one of the greatest spectacles seen locally; the burning oil from that fire spread all across the river and was seen for many miles. There was no way of putting it out, so it had to just be left to burn itself out. Even serious flooding from the River Avon in 1894 didn't close the plant. A very important company during both wars, their products were needed for the war effort, and they even had their own fire-watchers. It ended its days being owned by the British Steel Corporation.

Today, original cottages from the industrial days of the eighteenth and nineteenth centuries co-exist with the 'Quayside Village', built on the old tar works site. Although the heavy industry has gone, along with many buildings, the countryside character and narrow lanes of Crews Hole remain. It is an area rich in industrial and social history.

This picture, taken at St Anne's Slip, shows three boats out of the water for repairs and maintenance. The boat on the right has the number 129, and the words 'George Orse', or possibly 'Morse', and the name *Masia* can just be read. Troopers Hill is on the far right, and the chimneys and buildings to the left probably belonged to one of the Fireclay works.

Crews Hole looking towards Butler's tar works. In the foreground, modern warehouse units have been built along the banks of the River Avon. The tar works was originally established in 1843 and closed in 1980. On the opposite side of the river to the right is the St Anne's Board Mills, which date from 1913. This photograph was taken in April 1980, and five months later the closure of the whole mill was announced. The *Evening Post*'s front-page headline was 'Mill to Shut – 800 axed'.

The Lamb Inn is reported to be at least 300 years old. In the past the cellars were used as a mortuary for bodies dragged out of the river. It closed as a pub in late 1950s. The building is still there but boarded up, and has seen better days. The buildings to the left have all been demolished.

1953 coronation party. Bill Hares leads his family and local children from one side of the Lamb Inn. The Board Mills can be seen over the water. The kiln behind the children was once part of the Crews Hole Pottery, originally owned by Anthony Ammats, or Amatts. There were two kilns there at one time, and the firm made mugs for public houses, jugs, household cups, bowls and chamber pots which were usually sold from a horse and cart around the streets of East Bristol.

Street party. We believe that this picture was taken in 1953, probably to celebrate the coronation, in Fir Tree Lane, with members of Crews Hole chapel in attendance. Can you name anyone?

A picture taken in 1980: the Lamb Inn had closed years before. It had an alternative use for some time but now stands boarded up.

The Lamb Inn with its gas lamp, and a horse and cart outside. The horses have left a few 'messages' along the road. Everything to the left has now been demolished. The picture was taken by Dr Fryer, who we assume was the local doctor.

Left: Cottages close to the Lamb Inn in around 1900: they have all since been demolished. The residents pose for the camera. The baby is well wrapped up with a bonnet on. Photograph by Dr Fryer.

Below: The local residents are seen at their coronation party in 1953, held in the garden of the Lamb Inn. A few children shade their eyes from the sun. Mary Sheppard's family is present.

The Wesleyan church at Crews Hole was built by Charles Smith, a mason who worked at the cotton factory in Barton Hill. The chapel measured just 35ft by 24ft. Archibald Vickers, the works manager at the cotton factory, laid the foundation stone in September 1860. It closed during the last war and has been incorporated into an engineering works.

Displaced Person. Filming started in early 1985, but it was three years before it reached our screens. *Displaced Person*, made by HTV, was set in Germany. A young orphaned black boy is brought up by nuns. The first black man he meets is a GI sergeant and the boy convinces himself that the soldier is his father. The film starred Stan Shaw and Swindon boy Julius Gordon. A shanty town was recreated at Crews Hole. Filming also took place at other locations in the west. It won an Emmy award in America. Seen here is a local resident, Alice Weymouth, on the set of the 1985 production.

HTV LIMITED, THE TELEVISION CENTRE, BATH ROAD, BRISTOL BS4 3HG. TELEPHONE 0272 778366 TELEX 44156

TELEPHONE

10th January 1985

THE RESIDENTS
Crews Hole Road Area

"D.P." - A New Drama for Television from H.T.V.

From 14th January until 16th January 1985 we will be filming scenes in
Crews Hole for "D.P.", a television film about post-war G.I.s in Germany.

The Police and Local Authorities have been fully informed of our
arrangements and we hope that, despite the bad weather, you will enjoy
our stay without inconvenience.

If you require any further information, please do not hesitate to contact
me at the Production Office, HTV West Ltd, on Bristol 778366.

Thank you.

Left: An HTV letterhead.

Below: A drawing of
Crews Hole cottages, *c.*
1913, by Samuel Loxton.

Coal digging on Troopers Hill. The market gardens are on the other side. Troopers Hill is now covered with grass and trees. The gardens have been replaced by houses.

One of Bristol's great artists was Samuel Loxton. This is his drawing of Crews Hole Road. Note the colliery engine house on the corner of Troopers Hill Road.

Left: The stack, Troopers Hill Road. This square chimney is all that remains of the colliery engine house, which was built of Pennant rubble with copper-slag dressings. A by-product of quarrying, mining and industrial processes, slag was commonly used in the Crews Hole area. In 1896 two small coal mines were recorded in Crews Hole. One was called Troopers Hill and the other Blackswarth Hill Mine. The stack is now listed as being of historical significance.

Below: Crews Hole Methodist church. Built in 1853, it closed on 13 September 1987. It has since been converted into flats. In its early days, gas, and later electricity, was supplied by Butler's, and later again by British Steel until they closed in 1981. On 4 September 1982 its one and only marriage took place: Susan Lawrence and Roy Annis wanted to marry in that chapel, but in order to do so, they had to hire a generator for power and a safe to keep the documents in (a legal requirement).

1853-1978

✠ Crews Hole Methodist Church ✠

125th Anniversary Celebrations

Saturday & Sunday 1st & 2nd April, 1978

THY WAY O GOD IS IN THE SANCTUARY

Above: The interior of Crews Hole Methodist church. This picture was taken in 1987 during its final days as a church.

Left: This picture is entitled 'Belgium in Bristol', but to us it is Crews Hole. Text on the reverse reads: 'This picture was hung in the Seventh Annual Western International Photographic Salon held at Bristol England in 1935.' The photographer was possibly Muchamore of Lawrence Hill.

An unusual 1960s view from Crews Hole looking across Butler's Tar Works to St Anne's Board Mills. The Barton Hill flats dominate the skyline.

The great unloading shed at St Anne's Board Mills awaits demolition in September 1983. The last barges were unloaded in the mid-1960s. After that the pulp came by rail from Portishead to Marsh Ponds and then by road the short distance to St Anne's.

September 1983: demolition is well under way at the vast St Anne's Board Mills site. It is a far cry from 1966 when the company won a Queen's Award for Industry. The St Anne's Board Mills were internationally known and had a very high reputation. However in October 1980 they closed as the economic recession intensified.

The largest and newest of the Board Mills chimneys, the 300ft tall giant was the last to go, and in dramatic style. During 1982-83 it was reduced in height and then the date was fixed for its spectacular exit. A large crowd gathered on all vantage points on the morning of Sunday 12 August 1984. A hooter sounded, explosive charges were let off and the vast stack toppled over, breaking into two as it crashed down to earth. The dust settled on the Avon turning it brick red. The last of the area's giant chimneys was no more.

Right: Dundridge House, *c.* 1910, the home of the Drake family, now demolished. Fernwood off Dundridge Lane now stands in its place.

Below: The Drake family, 1910. From left to right, back row: Mary Ann Drake (*née* Dark) with baby Edna May, Guido (known as Jake), Rose Elizabeth, Plimsole Redford, May, Guido Drake (Father). George and Victor are sitting in front. Guido was a market gardener with $2\frac{1}{2}$ acres and also the local lamplighter for Crews Hole and Brislington. Summer started at 10 p.m. for him – when he finished he had his breakfast before turning them all off.

Left: Haymaking in Nibletts Hill Field, 1928. On the left are Edward Weymouth and Herbert Francombe, while at the far right is Walter Hicks, the local milkman who had a cottage near to the Bull public house. The children include Bill Towzer.

Below: The Marquis of Worcester off-licence on the corner of Corkers Hill. The original owners, the Rogers family, once worked for the Duke of Beaufort who gave permission to use one of his family titles. Alice Weymouth, who was related to the Rogers, ran this place until 1991. She once applied for an indoor licence, but it was opposed by the nearby Bull pub. The building still stands today.

Edward Weymouth, owner of the Marquis of Worcester, with his daughter, Alice, beside the off-licence, *c.* 1928. He also had a bakery attached to that building. After he baked the bread he and his son would deliver it around the district. The van took the place of the horse and cart seen below.

The writing on the cart says 'E. Weymouth – Baker – St George'. Edward's son, also Edward, aged about eleven, gets ready to start work. The photograph was taken outside the off-licence in around 1921.

One of the best-known boats at Crews Hole was the *Carbolate*, belonging to Butler's. Here she is tied up at Butler's Tar Works in the 1920s. The *Carbolate* was a motor barge built in 1911. She transported liquids between Crews Hole and Gloucester Docks. Thankfully she has been restored somewhere in the Midlands.

The crew of the *Carbolate* at Butler's Tar Works in the mid-1920s. Second from the right is Jim Sweet and at extreme left is Stanley White. Other barges in the fleet included *Jean, Jolly*, and *Darby*.

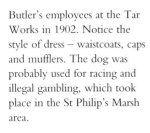

Butler's employees at the Tar Works in 1902. Notice the style of dress – waistcoats, caps and mufflers. The dog was probably used for racing and illegal gambling, which took place in the St Philip's Marsh area.

In 1970 ownership of Butler's Tar Works passed to the British Steel Corporation. Work ceased in 1980 after a disastrous fire. The site has since been redeveloped with private houses, after a lot of money was spent decontaminating the site. These pictures are from the British Steel days.

William Butler & Co. converted from barges to road transport in the 1950s. This ex-military International articulated tanker, of which Butler's had a fleet, is seen loading at Crews Hole.

This AEC Mammoth Major eight-wheeled tanker is seen at the Crews Hole works in British Steel Corporation days. This, vehicle delivered in 1973, has a standard ergomatic cab which AEC, Albion and Leyland shared.

British Steel Corporation also operated Leyland articulated tankers such as this one delivered in 1971. This vehicle also has an Ergomatic cab.

Rear view of a Leyland articulated tanker, delivered in 1971. This tanker appears to be in pristine condition and has probably just been delivered.

St Aidan's church, known as Little St Aidan's, opened in 1880 and closed in 1905. The school house was next door. Butler's bought both buildings and used them as research labs. Both were later demolished. The font and other furnishings went to Big St Aidan's at St George.

Thomas Iles at Butler's Tar Works in the 1890s. Thomas is standing at the far right. He worked in the cooperage department making barrels.

Butler's tanks in 1972-73. The wall was where the mission church and schoolrooms once stood.

1972-73: part of Butler's, at this time a British Steel plant. In 1974, Tony Benn, the local MP and then Industry Secretary, closed the works as an emergency move after a creosote vapour leak and fire.

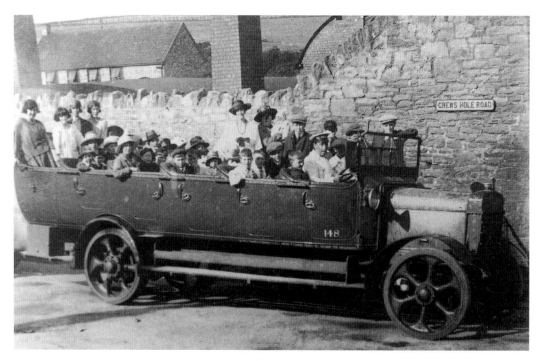

A charabanc outing setting off from Crews Hole Road in the 1920s. The charabanc belonged to Bristol Tramways and was built in the company's own workshops. Note the solid tyres.

The Conham Ferry, seen from Beese's tea garden, takes visitors across the water. The Crews Hole side is now completely changed, with trees and shrubbery hiding this view.

Dr Fryer's picture of 'The White Houses', Corkers Hill and Parfitts Hill. All have since been demolished. All the buildings seem to have seen better days.

Brand new buildings stand on the site of the houses in the previous picture. They may be new but they do seem to lack character. To the left, just by the garages, is the old off-licence, Marquis of Worcester.

Built on the site of Butler's football pitch and part of Conham Hall land, Conham sewage works opened in 1937. It served the southern part of Kingswood until 1968 when the sewer was extended to Avonmouth.

These workers were employed at Thatcher's Quarry in the 1920s and '30s. First on the left is Thomas Hicks (sitting), sixth from left is Aaron Hicks. The Hicks family were masons and worked on Cossham Hospital, Wesley Memorial church, St Aidan's church and Air Balloon school.

Thatcher's Quarry near the hundred steps in the 1920s. Tom Curtis (left) was still working when he was eighty years old. In early days there were probably twelve quarries operating between Conham and the Chequers Inn, employing between 200 and 400 men. They were all closed by the early 1930s.

These ruined buildings mark the site of a copper smelter which was established in 1696 and was the first to successfully smelt copper using coal as a fuel. Later the building housed a smelly chemical works processing animal waste products; they also made tallow candles for the local coal mines.

Crews Hole Band of Hope marching through Kingswood, *c.* 1936. George Perrett, Bill Smart, George Hicks and Jack Britton are among those pictured.

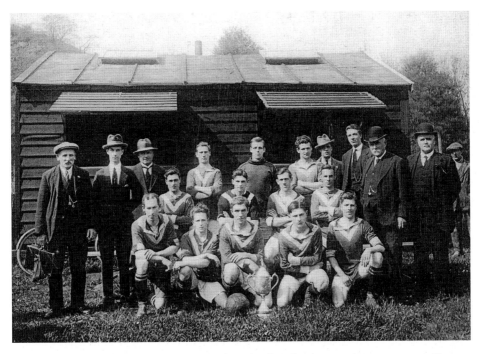

Butler's football team. We have no names and no date but they seem to have won a cup. Can anyone help with information?

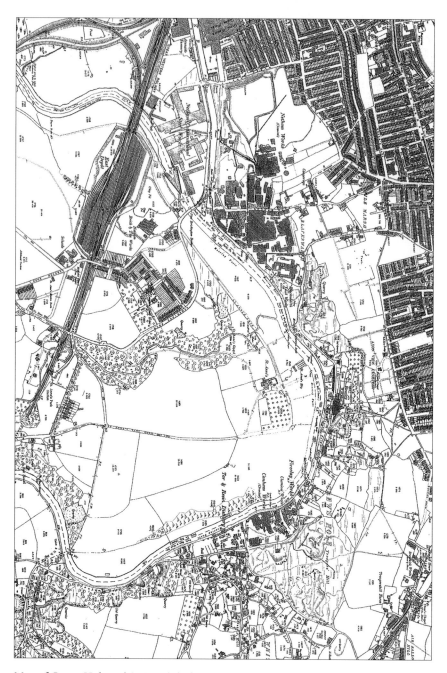

Map of Crews Hole and St Anne's before the building of St Anne's Board Mills and
St Anne's Housing Estate.

three

St George

Betty Hares says farewell to Salem church. The Revd Clutterbuck stands next to her.

Betty Hares 1921-99: Local Hero

'I could not have been very old, because our kitchen table was not very large, it only needed to accommodate four, my parents, my young sister and me. I was sitting comfortably underneath, the Bible storybooks open at a picture of the crucifixion, the tears rolling down my cheeks. I can still feel the pain; what it meant or where that picture would take me I could have no idea, but my bumpy journey had begun.'

The words of Betty Hares on how she discovered God.

She grew up in Seneca Street and attended Summerhill Infants' and Junior School before going on to St George Secondary School, but it was at the Salem Methodist chapel on Church Road that she heard visiting missionaries from Africa and decided that she wanted to serve God and be a missionary as well.

She trained as a nurse at the beginning of the Second World War, then in 1948 she went to China as a Methodist missionary nurse and only left because of the Communist revolution there. She also served in Africa. She returned to Bristol in 1981 where she taught at the Wesley Theological College and worked as an artist and poet.

She died on 8 July 1999 aged seventy-eight.

Above: Salem unemployment scheme, November or December 1932. In Salisbury Street the local unemployed repaint the church walls.

Right: The 38th Boys' Brigade outside what was Salem church on Church Road, *c.* 1957. Smith's auto shop is behind. Alex Roberts, later the Revd Roberts, and John West were both officers at that time. Beverley Harris and Lewis Lintern are just two of the boys.

St Patrick's church, Blackswarth Road, was founded by Father William Dillon and opened in 1923.

Mark Deacon, Church Road, in the 1960s. Mark opened this shop in 1947. Before that he had been a professional window dresser for Thorne Bros. Donald Speirs ran the shop for him from 1951 until it closed in 2001. In 1960 they were selling three dozen ties a week – the Fathers' Day display read 'A new tie is a tonic'.

The lake – the focal point of St George Park. Unlike Eastville's lake it was designed from the outset to be a key feature. It was also an expression of 'one-upmanship'. St George Park was initially the creation of the St George Council at a time when the St George area was outside Bristol. The lake and the design of St George Park in general was much more sophisticated than anything the Bristol Corporation had!

The bowling green in St George Park, pictured shortly after the green was laid out in June 1909. The tennis courts were to the left. On the horizon is St George's church, the rear of the original St George library and the Netham chemical works chimney.

The eastern end of the lake in the park, home to swans and ducks. Note the low fencing, which was removed in the 1970s. In the background are the houses of Clouds Hill Avenue and, on the left, the industrial structures based around the former 1801 St George poorhouse.

The St George Park lake held a fascination for generations of children. Here Edwardian children watch the swans and boats go by. Paddle boats, canoes and skiffs were an important ingredient of summer days in the park. Boating was foolishly axed in 1993.

An aerial view of St George Park showing Avon Tin Printers in the bottom right corner. St Ambrose church is at top right and St George School at top left.

A barrage balloon in St George Park during the Second World War, tethered by the old cricket and football pitch.

St George ARP in 1945. Mr Day the local curate is at far right with Bill Elliot next to him. The ARP service was then stationed in the old council building, now the Labour Club.

The Free Library, St George, was opened on 19 October 1898. In those days all books were listed: you selected your choice and the librarian collected that book for you. In 1921 it was reorganised and reopened on an open access system, where you selected your own books much as you do today.

Salem church. The annual fancy-dress parade with some very inventive costumes. Can anyone date this picture or name anyone?

Right: The Tramway Refreshment Rooms were owned by the Clements family. Drivers and conductors from the nearby Beaconsfield Road tram depot pose outside along with local children. It is still a café today, now next to the Labour Club.

Below: The interior of the tramway depot, Beaconsfield Road, St George, in 1939. The depot was built in 1876 as a terminus and stabling for horse-drawn trams. In the 1890s a generating station was built at the rear of the depot to power the new line to Kingswood. The sheds were demolished in 1987.

Above: The old Three Horseshoes pub on Church Road. It was rebuilt prior to the creation of the park in the 1890s. Later, the Park Cinema stood to the right. Elizabeth Britton was the owner and her family continued to run it well into recent times. The man standing sixth from the left is Thomas Phipps. Also present are Dr Gerrish and Mr Verrier, a local JP and tailor. The fifth man along on the coach was known as Big Betsy.

Right: An eighteenth-century bath house, two storeys high, with a façade three bays wide, defined by pilasters constructed with the blue-black copper slag blocks produced at Crews Hole, alternating with stucco brickwork. The doorway led you into the bath house where you could take a cold bath. The water came from a now defunct spring feeding a stone-walled reservoir nearby.

Opposite: Plan of the bath house, which was probably built by a Quaker, William Reeve, who also built Arnos Court, using the same materials. This bath house could at one time be seen from the riverside. There was also a terraced garden, later used as allotments but now completely engulfed by ivy and trees.

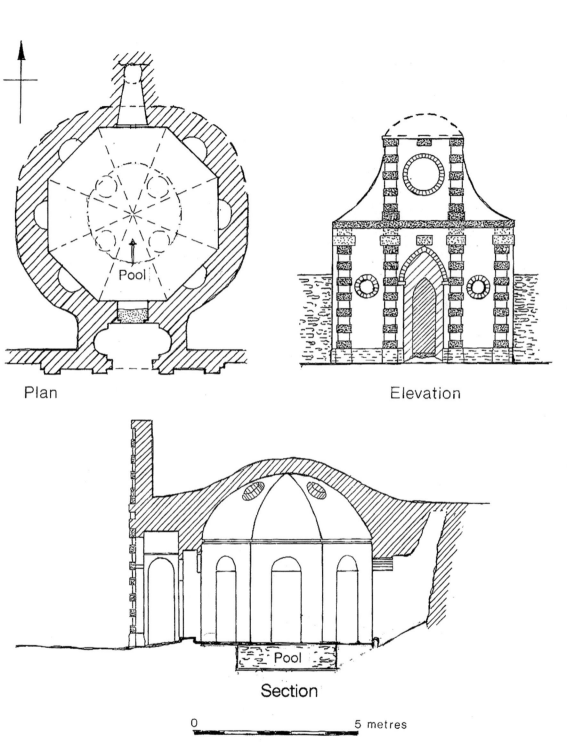

Plan

Elevation

Pool

Pool

Section

0   5 metres

The Phipps family, seen here in 1906, were market gardeners, masons and house builders. They built many of the streets in St George as well as the cemetery at Avon View and the Lodge, in front of which they are pictured. The parents were also the superintendents of the cemetery. From left to right, back row: Thomas, James, Robert, George. Front row: Annie, Polly (grandmother), Thomas (grandfather), Susannah and Bess.

The Lodge, Avon View Cemetery, St George, home of the Phipps family.

The Bennett family of Beaconsfield Road, 1914–15. This shows a good selection of early 1900s clothes: a soldier in the middle, Sidney Bennett in the trilby at the back, and children being well behaved for the family wedding.

Sidney Bennet Jr in the 1950s. He lived at No. 6 Beaconsfield Road, the corner house, which was also on Beaufort Road, opposite the cemetery. His father had started with a horse and cart – now they had a motor van.

Langridge's, 248A Church Road. The girls are making a presentation to Mr and Mrs Sheriff, owners of this corset and brassière factory, to mark their silver wedding anniversary in 1950. Singer sewing machines fill the room. Langridge's was in business back in the early 1850s and moved to Church Road around the turn of the century. Their goods were sold all round the world. Parachutes were made during the Second World War. Their products went out of fashion after this; they closed in the 1970s and moved back to Cornwall.

Opposite above: The fountain, St George, complete with drinking troughs. Local legend indicates that the fountain was the site of Don John's Cross (see *Images of England: St George, Redfield and Whitehall*, published by Tempus in 2001). Some historians suggest that the Cross could be associated with King John. Traditionally he is thought to have had a hunting lodge in the Kingswood Forest.

Opposite below: The post office at St George and, next door, Smith's the undertakers, *c.* 1920. St George parish church is in the background.

St George, Bristol.

St GEORGE'S POST OFFICE

St George Fountain from the garden of Clouds Hill House, looking towards the fountain memorial, before traffic lights were installed. A local policeman from St George police station stands on the corner of Church Road and Glebe Road.

Summerhill Infants' School nativity play, *c.* 1964. The school was built by the St George Local Board in 1877.

Summerhill Infants' School, 1919-20.

Summerhill Junior School class photograph, 1969. From left to right, back row: Mr Rule,
Yvonne Mead, Lynda Blackmore, Jill Payne, Susan Wiltshire, Christine Sheppard, Karen
Edwards, Mr Welch (headmaster). Second row: Ken Pang, Mark Jones, Frederick Jennings,
Martyn Escott, Daryl Hawkes, Martin Nash, Anthony Baldwin, Stephen Hudd, Barry Dursley.
Third row: Catherine Lismore, Julie Smith, Carol Williams, Jayne Baxter, Susan Miller, Denise
Shepherd, Karen Alderman, Rosalind Rowe. Front row: Peter Burrows, Nigel Ball, Paul
Hayward, Mark Dillon-Boylan, Martin Champion.

Bethel Chapel, Clouds Hill Road, in 1964. The original building still stands and is today in use as a fitness centre.

The interior of Bethel Chapel in 1964, showing the ornate altar railings and the balcony and organ at the front of the chapel. When the chapel was redesigned, the organ and balcony were moved to the rear of the chapel over the entrance.

The junction of Bell Hill Road and Clouds Hill Road, St George, on 21 August 1939. The Bristol Tramways electric tramcar No. 135 is passing the Tramway Tavern on its way to Old Market. On the right is the World End public house.

Until recently this building on Clouds Hill Road proudly proclaimed 'Tramway Tavern'. It was formerly an off-licence and closed many years ago. The name commemorated the electric tramway from Old Market to Kingswood which opened in 1895. Sadly it has recently been repainted. Another bit of east Bristol history has been lost.

H.H. Dark, motor engineer and taxi service at 19 Bell Hill Road, was advertised as the only taxi driver in St George and operated the first petrol station between Old Market and Kingswood. A modern petrol station now stands on this site, opposite Marling Road.

Dark's business entrance was in Bell Hill Road; this was the back way in, via Whiteway Road. The loft above had been used as a billiard room in the 1920s. The vehicle is a 1947 Singer 12.

Dark's cycle shop, 23 Bell Hill Road. The name Raleigh dominates the business – there are no foreign bikes as yet. The tyres are extremely thin compared with today's mountain bikes.

Members of Clowes Methodist church at the junction of Bell Hill Road and Bellvue Road, *c.* 1920. The Bell Hotel is in the distance on the left. The cottages and Ebenezer chapel on the right have since been demolished.

A Whitsuntide procession around 1930, including a group from Bethel chapel, at Rodney Road Sports Field where the procession ended with tea and games for the children. The man wearing the bowler hat, kneeling by the horse, is Mr Yeoman.

St George cricket team in the 1890s. From left to right, back row: Arthur Palmer, Harry Palmer, -?-, Mr Issacs, Edward Ware. Middle row: Mr Beard (Baptist minister), Tom Merrike, Bill Palmer. Front row: Fred Cannon, Mr Drake, -?-, -?-.

The shop of William Sampson, greengrocer and fruiterer at 139 Two Mile Hill Road, *c.* 1940. The Sampson family owned market gardens in the Footshill area of St George. Sampson's shop was in between Burchell's Green Road and King Street.

Above: St Aidan's, the original church known locally as the 'Iron Church', was dedicated on 21 May 1883. It was situated near the corner of Casseybottom Lane opposite Kennon Road.

Right: The interior of the old 'Iron Church', which was very cold during the winter. The congregation later moved up to the new St Aidan's on the top of Nags Head Hill.

Nags Head Hill, the site for the new St Aidan's church. The sign states 'Subscriptions urgently needed and thankfully received by F.T. Parker', who was in charge of the Crews Hole Mission.

St Aidan's as it was when dedicated in 1904. The cost was £6,591 12s. Note the overhead tram line.

The vicar of St Aidan's, we believe, with his son and local children. The houses are 102-126 Hillside Road. (Photograph by Dr Fryer)

The vicar of St Aidan's at the back of Hillside Road, Nos 80-86. The building on the left was used as stables and later a garage.

Taylor's corner shop, Nicholas Lane, near St Aidan's, in 1913-14. To the right is Harwood Road. Annie and Mary Taylor display their dolls for the cameraman.

Above: Tramcar No. 124 at the brow of Nags Hill, St George. Note the posters on the hoardings advertising the latest films at the Park Picture House and the Kingsway Cinema, both in St George.

Left: Number 93 Nags Head Hill. The Britannia off-licence and store was run by the Fink family for many years. In the 1920s about six houses further along from here were Blackboy and Trumpet Lane, now disappeared. This building has now been converted into a house.

The Air Balloon tavern, photographed when it belonged to Georges and Co. Ltd. It is still in operation, with just a bit of modernisation.

The Air Balloon School, 1954. From left to right, back row: Mr Warren, K. Abraham, Paul Britton, ? Hillier, Paul Oats, Michael Britton, Dave Bartlett, Roy Yeadon, Donald Haynes, Michael Loads. Second row: ? Sheppard, Phillip Tallboys, Jill Lawrence, ? Harding, -?-, Bernie Britton, Sheila Shride, ? Weight, John Newman, Michael Blake, Miss Bowden-Lyle. Third row: ? Struggle, -?-, Diane Schamel, -?-, -?-, -?-, ? Mitchell, -?-, -?-, -?-, -?-. Front row: Colin Chadwell, Phillip Scrase, Paul Wilmott.

Mr George White Snr, bandsman, cornet player and the founder of the Bristol East Reed and Brass Temperance Band. This photograph was taken in 1952 and he died the following year. The band was founded in 1892 and rehearsed for many years at Clowes chapel.

Bristol East Temperance Band, c. 1930. Second row from the back on the extreme left is Albert James, and fourth from the left is Edward James. On the front row, fifth from the right, is the bandmaster George White. The band originated at Clowes chapel but moved to the Wesley chapel when Clowes was demolished.

Summerhill Road in the late 1930s. To the left, out of sight, is the Pied Horse pub. To the right is Clovelly Road; the first shop is now Jones the Bakers. The previous owners were the Crews family. The buildings on the left were demolished for road widening; there were orchards behind.

Summerhill Porter Stores at 79 Summerhill Road on the corner of Bethel Road. The shop was part of a Victorian row called Clevedon Terrace. It was demolished in the 1960s to create green space around Butler House, a block of flats.

four

Speedwell

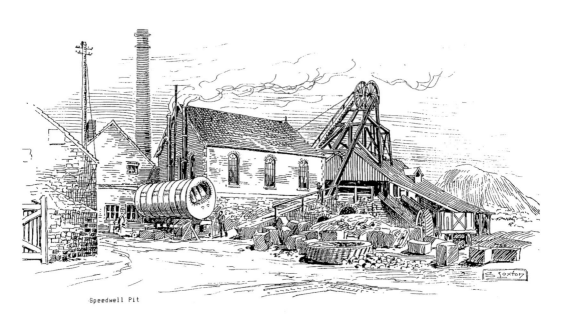

Speedwell Pit

Speedwell Pit in a drawing by Samuel Loxton.

The Speedwell area was once a part of the wild deer forest of Kingswood, but is now a well-populated area of Bristol housing several thousand people.

Extraction of coal began in the area in the early 1700s. By mid-Victorian times coal was in great demand by both Bristol householders and industrialists. By 1845 both the Speedwell Pit (then known as the Starveall Pit) and Deep Pit were in existence. Deep Pit was over 1200ft deep, supplying good-quality coal from the Great Vein.

The rest of the Speedwell area at that time consisted of a mixture of arable and pastureland. The three main farms were Speedwell Farm, Crofts End Farm and Holly Bush Farm. The Great Forest of Kingswood had long been cleared, leaving an area predominantly rural in nature but scarred in many places by the demands of the coal mining and the brick and tile industries.

The mines began to reach their full potential when they came into the ownership of Handal Cossham in 1861. Cossham introduced machinery worked by compressed air and within fifty years the supposedly exhausted pits were producing 210,000 tons of coal annually. Rows of cottages were built near the pits to house the miners, many of which are still standing to this day.

The Bristol house-building boom in late Victorian times fuelled the expansion of the second most important industry in the area, brick and tile making. The three principal makers were the Bristol Brick and Tile Works, Fussell's Brick and Tile Works and Hollybrook Brick Works.

After the First World War the council embarked on an ambitious project to build several estates of council houses in Bristol. One of these was established at Speedwell on land that had previously formed part of Speedwell Farm. Between 1920 and 1929 thirty-three acres of land was acquired from various landowners and streets of well-built council houses appeared.

However, all was not well with the local mining industry. In 1933 the people of Bristol contributed £3,000 towards new borings, to prevent the entire closure of the pits and the loss of 2,000 jobs. Two new tunnels were driven. However, it was not enough: the East Bristol Colliery Company lost a further £20,000 and on 3 April 1936 the last load of coal was brought to the surface.

The Speedwell housing estate was further expanded both before and after the war. Other facilities such as shops, the swimming baths, the clinic and Speedwell School were built. The old colliery buildings disappeared for the construction of the new Speedwell fire station and private housing was also built. The brick-making industry fared much better and survived into the early sixties.

Today Speedwell is a mainly residential area. The old brick-making quarries have been filled in to provide much-needed playing fields. As we write this, the old Speedwell TA barracks are being redeveloped with new houses providing a contrast with the traditional miners' cottages, pre-war council houses and post-war prefabs.

Memories of the Speedwell area

by David Cheesley

Before I started school at Speedwell the only thing I knew about the area was that it had a swimming bath. We went there for swimming lessons from Whitehall Junior School – not by bus but on foot, in all winds and weathers. That was to change when I received a letter in the summer of 1964 telling me that I had been offered a place at Speedwell Boys' School. As I had passed the 11-plus I was placed in the grammar stream. Speedwell was one of the first schools in Bristol to be converted from secondary modern to comprehensive. On the first day I caught the No. 13 bus from Whitehall Road and got off at the bus stop just before Speedwell fire station. School uniform was compulsory and even at that time some of the new boys were wearing caps and short trousers.

Speedwell Boys' School was modern and had extensive playgrounds and playing fields. Adjoining the school was Duncombe Lane. On the other side of Duncombe Lane was a disused quarry, which had water at the bottom, estimated to be about 40ft deep. This was a magnet to us boys. We played there at dinner times until one boy slipped down the side, broke his arm and probably would have drowned if he had fallen in the water. From then on boys were banned from going onto the quarry site. However, within a year the quarry was used as a tip for Bristol's rubbish, until it was completely filled in and levelled.

Swimming lessons were held at Speedwell Bath, first lesson Monday mornings. My memories are of waiting outside on the steps for the baths to open on freezing winter mornings. The bath itself in those days had diving boards and a springboard. I learnt to swim there and was awarded my four lengths certificate. Every year Speedwell School held an inter-house swimming gala. I represented Colston House in the breaststroke and relay races.

Just along from the swimming bath, past the TA centre, was Speedwell Clinic. We went there to see the dentist. I don't know her name, but the woman we saw must have hated children. She never gave any injections so you can imagine how painful a visit could be. No wonder so many Speedwell pupils hated going to the dentist.

Next to the clinic were the remains of a disused railway bridge. Being interested in railways, I discovered that it used to take the line from Speedwell Colliery to the Midland Railway line at Kingswood Junction. One dinner time my friends and I walked along the overgrown track bed as far as Foundry Lane Bridge. Other days we would walk down Holly Lodge Road, which at that time felt very rural. In one field were ponies, which we fed and got very fond of. There was also a pig farm situated about halfway along and in the valley was a stream, which we were always trying to dam. Some days we walked as far as the railway lines, in time to see the *Devonian* go up, before heading back to school.

Adjoining our playground was Speedwell fire station. As we played football at break times, we would see the new trainees being put through their paces, hosing out fires and rescuing casualties from the big tower. Smoke and flames were always in evidence. Several times a week the fire engines would roar out of the station on real emergencies. I particularly remember one bad winter, when deep snow was around, we had a snowball fight with the firemen, through the wire fence that separated us. One fireman was nearly knocked out by a stone hidden inside a snowball. Not thrown by me, by the way.

Left: In 1845 Speedwell Pit was known as Staveall Pit. By 1890 when this photograph was taken, it had turned into a big complex. On the left of the picture is the steam-driven winding house. Loaded coal wagons are ready to be taken over the Midland railway line to Bristol. Wooden pit props are strewn everywhere. The pit closed in 1936.

Below: Plan of Deep Pit and Speedwell Pit.

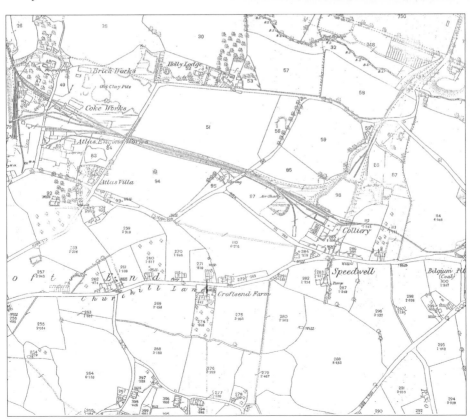

Speedwell Pit miners' voluntary rescue association in the early 1920s. These men trained in their own time and received no payment for their services. From left to right, back row: J.S. Moore (superintendent), A. Crew, A. Angell, H. Pitman, F. Beese, F. Crew (captain), S. Parker. Front row: F. Coates, G. Jones, J. Jefferies, W. Cox (captain). H. Pitman's job at other times was as an overman and shot-firer: he handled explosives, placing and detonating them in order to open up new seams.

Opposite: Part of the former Speedwell and Parkfield Colliery was sold by auction in 1900 to the Bedminster, Easton, Kingswood and Parkfield Collieries Ltd. Here it is on sale again in 1914.

Bedminster, Easton, Kingswood & Parkfield Collieries.
LIMITED.

Plans, Particulars and Conditions of Sale of the
Valuable and well-known Collieries of the above Company.

AT KINGSWOOD.

The SPEEDWELL COLLIERIES. with BELGIUM SHAFT and the DEEP PIT COLLIERY, together with the Extensive

FREEHOLD MINERALS,
about 1600 acres in extent,
with
Extensive Coke Works, Buildings and Numerous Cottages.

AT PUCKLECHURCH,
The Valuable Parkfield Collieries,
with Freehold Mineral area of **about 400 acres.**

also the LAND at SOUTH PIT, with numerous Cottages attached.

AT HANHAM.

THE INTEREST in the VALUABLE PIT known as

HANHAM COLLIERY,
with Leasehold Mineral area of **about 1,400 acres.**

PIECES OF VALUABLE BUILDING LAND,
at FEEDER ROAD, ST. PHILIP'S, with Siding to the North Somerset Railway Line, and at Easton part of the old Easton Colliery.

ACCOMMODATION LAND,
almost adjoining the land at Feeder Road, in St. Philip's Marsh, on the West side of the River Avon,

ACCOMMODATION or BUILDING LAND,
with Long Frontages to the roads leading to St. George, opposite the Speedwell Colliery; which

GEO. NICHOLS, YOUNG HUNT & Co.

will SELL BY AUCTION on

Thursday, August 13th. 1914, at 3 o'clock,
at the GRAND HOTEL, BROAD ST., BRISTOL.

Plans, Particulars and Conditions of Sale may be obtained from the Auctioneers, Demerara House, Colston Avenue, Bristol; or of

Messrs. Gibson & Ashford, 39 Waterloo Street, Birmingham.

Messrs. Johnson & Co, Solicitors, 36, Waterloo Street, Birmingham.

Mr. G. C. Rallison, Solicitor, 2 Bristol Chambers, Nicholas Street, Bristol.

The Deep Pit by Samuel Loxton. The numerous slag heaps surrounding the pit became popular with local children as unofficial playgrounds.

Deep Pit was in existence before 1845. This photograph from 1890 gives a good view of the winding machinery. The head frame stood 30ft high and the pulleys were 13ft in diameter. A line of Midland Railway wagons is seen being loaded and on the right are two local coal hauliers. The pit closed in 1936.

The Belgium pit house stands next to the workings of the Belgium pit. This house, on the corner of Whiteway Road, still stands next to the Duncombe Road parade of shops.

A fancy-dress parade outside Speedwell School in 1953. The marchers are turning into Duncombe Lane, possibly returning to Argyle Hall.

Duncombe Road. St. George. A7454

This row of shops was built in Duncombe Road in 1929 to serve the new Speedwell housing estate. Note the lack of traffic and the gas street lighting. The shops provided all the local needs and included a post office. In the distance are the houses of Sunny Bank, originally built as part of the Rodney Road council estate.

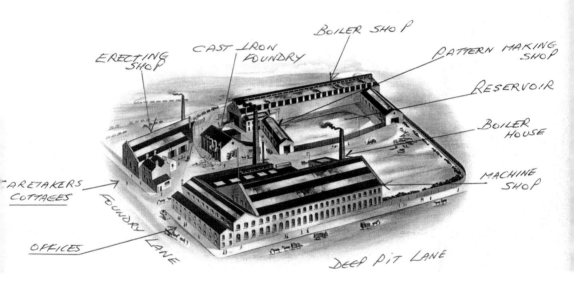

BOILER SHOP

CAST IRON FOUNDRY

ERECTING SHOP

PATTERN MAKING SHOP

RESERVOIR

BOILER HOUSE

CARETAKERS COTTAGES

FOUNDRY LANE

MACHINE SHOP

OFFICES

DEEP PIT LANE

Fox, Walker and Co. established the Atlas Locomotive Works at Deep Pit Road in 1864. The works was taken over by Thomas Peckett and Sons in 1880. Between 1864 and 1961, when the works closed, a total of 2,166 locomotives were built.

The boiler shop, where boilers and saddle tanks were made. On the right is the coppersmiths' shop, and the building by the chimney is the brass foundry. The old tracks lead to the old Speedwell Colliery – the line ran across Whitefield Road.

The erecting shop, where all the components were put together.

June 1965. The area had a number of brick and tile works. The Hollybrook Brick Co. Ltd occupied a large area bounded by Argyle Road, Whitefield Road, Duncombe Lane and Charlton Road. By 1944 the firm was known as Hollychrome Bricks Ltd. In 1957 Bristol Corporation purchased a large part of the site and from 1965 the quarry site was gradually filled in with household rubbish. After levelling it was grassed over. Note Argyle church on the right in the distance.

A street party held to celebrate the end of the Second World War in 1945. Mr Ham the caretaker of Speedwell School is pictured with David Gore, Brian Gore, Terry Gay, Mabel Huntley, Pat Huntley, Pauline Marsh, John Gay, Len Gore, David Heddrell, Ruth Strandle, J. Heddrell, Mrs Cameron and Maria Cameron.

Speedwell Swimming Baths, Whitefield Road, were opened in 1937 and were identical to the Jubilee Baths in Knowle. The 1930s saw real progress in swimming provision in the city and these baths were, and remain, a big asset for the Speedwell area. The building of public community baths dates back to the passing of the Baths and Wash Houses Act of 1850.

Opposite above: The interior of Speedwell Baths, a typically uncluttered 1930s design. The actual pool measures 75ft by 30ft. The baths are situated in Whitefield Road, named after Alderman William Whitefield. He was a popular miners' leader and city councillor. Before the house-building of the 1930s, Whitefield Road consisted of little more than a few cottages and an off-licence called the Old England Tavern.

Opposite below: Speedwell Clinic was built in 1937. The building was converted to a day centre for the mentally handicapped in 1985. By 2002 the building had been closed and boarded up.

Speedwell TA Centre was opened in 1940 and demolished in 2002, except for this building, which was totally gutted, had a new roof added and was converted into flats.

Speedwell TA Centre. All the other buildings have been demolished, including the old barrack buildings, seen here. Modern housing units have been built in their place.

Speedwell TA Centre. An unfortunate outcome of the modernisation of the main TA building is that the 'Territorial Army' wording and '1940' signs have been taken away.

Holly Lodge, a grand house built amongst the meadows, orchards and lanes of east Bristol, was famous as the home of Handel Cossham, the Victorian colliery owner and MP for Bristol East. Deep Pit was not far to the west, with Speedwell Pit a short walk to the south east. Locals knew the adjacent fields as 'The Gozzy' (see map on page 87).

Holly Lodge Road – not so much a road as a narrow 'country lane' in deepest Speedwell. On the immediate left is the site of Holly Lodge House. Off to the right were old clay pits while to the north is the Coombe Brook. Much new housing has been built in the area but enough of the old Holly Lodge Road remains to give an indication of what it was like in the Victorian days.

Speedwell School opened in 1933 and was built on land that was formerly part of Speedwell Colliery. In 1956 an extension to Speedwell School was built, which became Speedwell Boys' School. The original school then became Speedwell Girls' School. Before that the girls occupied the top floor and the boys the bottom floor. The girls' school was destroyed by fire in 1974; temporary buildings sufficed for many years until a new building was opened.

Speedwell Boys' School is the three-storey building on the right of this picture. It is typical of the glass, brick and steel schools built all over the country at that time. The newer building to the left is the sixth form block built in 1968. The sixth form had previously occupied a couple of classrooms on the top floor of the boys' school.

Speedwell Boys' School teachers pose in July 1963. On the front row, centre, with hands on knees is Mr G.L. Hall, the headmaster, known affectionately as 'Nobby Hall' by the boys. To his left, with arms folded, is Stratford Hall, the Deputy Head. Of the thirty-eight teachers only five are women. The photograph was taken on the grass outside the school hall at the end of the 1962/63 school year.

Speedwell school hall. The school hall at Speedwell was built in 1956 and was shared by both the girls' and boys' schools. On the extreme left is the shared dining hall. Behind the windows at the back is the headmaster's office of the boys' school. The hall had an impressive stage on which many plays and shows were performed. In the 1960s school milk was served in the hall at breaktimes. On Friday evenings it was used for detentions.

The latest school magazine is on sale in the girls' school, 1956. Note the fashions: sandals, white socks, full skirts, cardigans, white shirts and ties; no make up, no jewellery and sensible hair styles. How times have changed. Miss Adams was the headmistress at this time; among the teachers were Miss Fear, Miss Allen, Miss Thomas, Mrs Bone and Miss Mahoney.

This house, 321 Speedwell Road, belonged to Arthur George Hobbs, coal merchant. The house was surrounded on three sides by Speedwell School playground. One of the hazards of playing football in the playground was that the ball would sometimes go over the fence into Mr Hobbs' garden.

At the junction of Speedwell Road and Whitefield Avenue stood 281 Speedwell Road, a grey stone miners' cottage. On the extreme right is the wall of Speedwell Colliery. This cottage was demolished in September 1975 for road widening; Roegate House and new housing can be seen in the background. A Minor 1000 and Ford Anglia complete the scene.

The miners' cottage from behind; the colliery wall is visible on the left, with the Empress Coaches building and the tower of Speedwell fire station in background. The cottage is ready for demolition most of the roof tiles have already disappeared.

Speedwell fire station was opened officially by the Lord Mayor in April 1952. It was a four-bay fire station known as No. 6 by Bristol Fire Brigade. Late in 1974, it became B6 when it came under the County of Avon, and since 1 April 1996 it has been part of the Avon Fire Brigade.

A wartime turntable ladder vehicle, GLW424, in the process of giving a demonstration for the Home Office at Speedwell.

Private Potter was born in 1893 at a small cottage in Burchell Green Road, Speedwell. Although he had eight sisters, he was the only son. He was employed at Wills tobacco factory in Ashton until he enlisted in the 1st 4th Gloucester Regiment, C Company and was sent to France where he was injured. He returned home but died of his injuries, aged just twenty-two. He was engaged, and his fiancée never subsequently married. *Above:* The grave of Alfred Potter, which is on the south side of St Michael on the Mount, on the junction of the Kingsway. Until a few years ago his last living sister tended his grave.

Private Potter's coffin is escorted to the church, on one of about eight postcards produced to record the event. This was first military funeral of his regiment in Bristol.

Local man Frank Gore poses for the camera in Duncombe Lane, June 1954. The old school is to the right, with Speedwell Road in the distance.

Duncombe Lane is an almost empty road in June 1954, with just a moving bicycle and a lorry parked at the bottom. This picture was taken looking the opposite way to the top picture, towards the Hollybrook brick works.

Kingsmead Walk, Speedwell Housing Estate. Between 1920 and 1929 Bristol Corporation acquired 33 acres of land to build the estate. The houses on the estate are various types consisting of grey stone (Speedwell Road), red brick (Green Croft) and Bath stone (Kingsmead Walk). The Bath stone houses are seen in this photograph and still look very smart over seventy years later.

The council houses along Speedwell Road facing the school and the fire station are made of grey stone. Many houses on the estate are of the same design as these but are constructed of red brick. Unusual houses built in Telford Walk in 1926 were made of steel and known as the Telford type. Light blue in colour, they were demolished in 1972 and replaced with traditional red-brick designs.

After the Second World War, house building was a major priority. In 1946 Bristol Corporation purchased $6\frac{1}{2}$ acres of land from Messrs Maggs Bros. On the site the corporation built fifty-four prefabs, such as these on Mallard Close. The prefabs were only meant to be temporary but have so far lasted fifty-six years.

The living room in one of the Mallard Close prefabs in the late 1940s or early 1950s. There was no television in those days and the radio takes pride of place.

On 27 June 1928 Bristol Corporation acquired 3 acres of land from William H. Watkins to build Crown Hill Estate. These fine houses were built on the estate.

The University Settlement purchased land and buildings that were formerly part of Speedwell Colliery on Speedwell Road in 1947. The first activities took place in this Nissen hut and the cottage behind. An enforced move to new premises at Whiteway Road took place in 1951 as the site was required for the new Speedwell fire station.

The new University Settlement building at Whiteway Road opened in 1951. There was a subsequent loss of support at first as the new building was situated on the other side of Speedwell Housing Estate. The building is still standing.

The Lady Mayoress of Bristol opens the New University Settlement Hall at Whiteway Road in 1951.

Above: 'Cold War Shadow' over Speedwell: the Civil Defence surface blockhouse at the corner of Brook Road and Crofts End Road. It was a hardened command and control centre, one of four built in Bristol in 1954. It was demolished in December 1997 exactly ten years after the historic Washington summit meeting between Ronald Reagan and Mikhail Gorbachev.

Right: 1950s Civil Defence Corps arm bands as worn by local volunteers. The CDC was on the highest state of alert during the Cuban missile crisis of October 1962. The organisation was disbanded in 1968.

George Brown 1875-1949

George Brown was born in 1875 in Somerset. He came to Bristol with his father, looking for work, in 1889. They would both find jobs at the Deep Pit colliery in Speedwell.

At the age of eighteen, George made a commitment to the Church. He would attend many meetings, a lot of them in the open air, preaching the Gospel. He gained a following which grew and grew, and his flock raised the money to build their own chapel. This was erected by fellow miners before and after their shifts.

The chapel opened on 8 July 1908. The miners even formed their own brass band which played on this occasion. The miners played a big part in the history of this chapel: they were even allowed to use it when on strike in 1911.

George died on 23 February 1949. Hundreds of people attended his funeral, including the Lord Mayor.

George Brown's grave, tended by his wife Blanch, Gwennie Brown, the wife of George's son Douglas, and her daughter Jennifer.

Number 13 Speedwell Road, the home of the Coles family. George Brown lived next door (No. 11) to that house, in Crofts End Road.

William Jesse Cox, aged twenty-seven, had permission to leave work early to join his wife at Weston-Super-Mare. He went up from Deep Pit in a cage without gates, and somehow he fell out and died of massive head injuries. His wife heard about the accident when a newspaper boy was selling papers on the beach shouting 'Disaster at Bristol Coal Mine'. Inside was her husband's name. William was a member of the Crofts End Mission, a Sunday School teacher and bandsman. Here his colleagues walk beside his coffin in June 1923. This is Whitehall Road with Rose Green School in the background.

A recent view of Crofts End Mission.

Winifred Phillips and Alma Taylor lead the primary class at Crofts End in the mid-1940s.

Crofts End Sunday School anniversary, 1940s. Dorothy Grant (née Brown) and her son Michael are pictured. They emigrated to Australia.

The Crofts End Band in Old Chapel, with George Brown's memorial stone in the background, in the early 1950s. In the picture are Bill Palfrey, Norman Palfrey, Fred Phillips, Stan Brown, Dennis Brown (trombone), and Phillip Brown. The conductor was Bill Brown (George Brown's son).

Phone 20021

24/2/49

THE MANSION HOUSE,
Clifton. Bristol.

Dear Mrs Brown.

Please allow me to offer
my Condolences to you at
the passing away of your
Dear Husband and my
Friend "George".

He was a friend to me;
because he endeavoured to
be a "friend to all".

I appreciate that my
name is linked with his in
this evening papers; as I
still hear testimony to his
honourableness.

You and your children
have lost a kindly husband,
and a Worthy Father! You know
however he is now at rest
after his long illness. May
You be given Divine strength
to bear your loss; is the
Sympathetic wish of
Yours Sincerely
Mrs G. Brown &
Family
Speedwell. Bristol 5.
Pres. C. Gill
Lord Mayr.

Above: Crofts End Mission
Silver Band, August 1926.
Many of its members were
local miners.

Left: A letter to George
Brown's wife from the Lord
Mayor of Bristol, Charles Gill,
dated 1949.

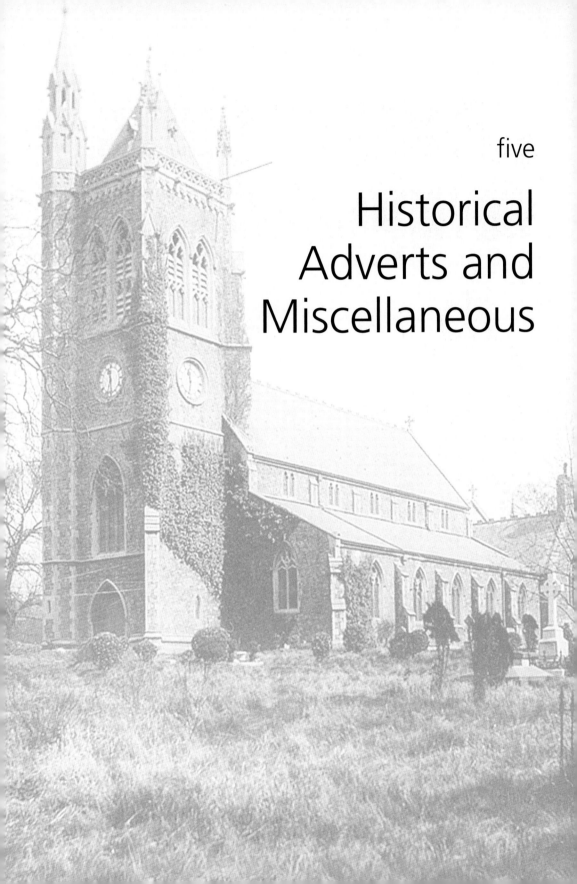

five

Historical
Adverts and
Miscellaneous

Swimming bath regulations.

ALL COMMUNICATIONS TO BE ADDRESSED TO THE FIRM AND NOT TO INDIVIDUALS.

CODES USED
A.B.C. (ENGINEERING) 5TH ED
BENTLEYS, MARCONI.

TELEGRAMS:
PECKETT, BRISTOL.
PECKLOCOMO, SOWEST, LONDON

TELEPHONES:
FISHPONDS, BRISTOL: 55346/7
LONDON, ABBEY 2813

ALL QUOTATIONS ARE SUBJECT TO STRIKE, ACCIDENT &c. CLAUSES AND
LOCOMOTIVES IN STOCK OR IN PROGRESS ARE OFFERED SUBJECT TO BEING UNSOLD

PECKETT & SONS LTD
LOCOMOTIVE ENGINEERS

London Office:
9, VICTORIA STREET
WESTMINSTER, S.W.1

Mr. E.T.Taylor,
13, Speedwell Road,
St.George,
BRISTOL.5.

ATLAS LOCOMOTIVE WORKS,
ST GEORGE,
BRISTOL. 5.

Date   8th. June 1953.

Our Ref.   WTP/EL.

Your Ref.

Dear Sir,

We thank you for your letter and are pleased
to hear you are celebrating your 58th Anniversary on
Saturday and Sunday 13th and 14th. June.

We have pleasure in enclosing cheque for
ten shillings and hope this will be of some little help
to you.

Yours faithfully,
Peckett & Sons, Limited.

Wilfred T. Peckett

Director.

Enclos.

A letter to an employer from Mr Peckett on Mr Taylor's fifty-eighth wedding anniversary in 1953.

G. E. & A. E. FUSSELL,
CROFTS' END
BRICK AND TILE WORKS,
ST. GEORGE, BRISTOL.

PLASTIC BRICKS, FLOORING & COPING SQUARES, DOUBLE
ROMAN & ANGLE TILES, Plain and Ornamental Crease.

Fussell's advertisement in a 1900 street directory. Their address was Brook Road, Crofts End, and they were still in business until the late 1940s.

Above and below: The Bristol Fire Clay Co., Blackswarth. The advertisements come from a *Wright's Directory* of the 1880s.

A 1900 advertisement for the Bristol Brick and Tile Co. from a street directory.

Hollybrook Brick Company Ltd advertisement from 1900.

St George parish church. The 1880 church was an impressive local landmark. Note the very large graveyard. Many lead coffins were discovered during the demolition of this structure in 1976.

The interior of St George church decorated for a harvest festival.

Left: A spooky picture of St George parish church. At this time the building was derelict, awaiting demolition.

Below: St George vicarage. The church was off to the left. Note the tennis court; there were also large well-tended pleasure gardens.

ST. GEORGE'S VICARAGE.

The park and the lake in an Edwardian picture looking towards Park Crescent. Note the mobile boating hut and the vast Whitehall Co-op bakery in the background.

One block of St Ann's Board Mill under construction.

St George school, opened in 1894 by the St George Council (not Bristol). A pioneering school, highly respected through the years.